I0436030

Design & Concepts L.L.C
April Issue 2014

House of
Lisabeth Design
<u>Magazine</u>

Today's Issue:

- *Doggy's world*
- *Fashion No's*
- *Design or Not*
- *Featured Business*

House of Lisabeth Design Magazine 2014

Health Watch

Health Trends: What We Know And What You Need To Know

Feet Fungus: Problems with foot health

Your feet the most important thing to you. Its what gets you around on ay to day basis. It's the way you feel in the morning and at night. Your feet's health is critical to having a good day and her we wanted to investigate the how's and how's of good feet health. (Fun fact most Americans spend 75,000 miles on there feet by the time they reach 50 years old.) Some tips for general health is yours shoes. You want to select shoes that are comfortable and can wear on a daily basis. Another tip is pedicures you want to keep up on pampering your feet so they don't wear out on you. "You can detect everything from diabetes to nutritional deficiencies just by examining the feet," says Jane Andersen, DPM, president of the American Association of Women Podiatrists and a spokeswoman for the American Podiatric Medical Association. The lowly left and right provide plenty of insightful data: Together they contain a quarter of the body's bones, and each foot also has 33 joints; 100 tendons, muscles, and ligaments; and countless nerves and blood vessels that link all the way to the heart, spine, and brain.

Unresolved foot problems can have unexpected consequences. Untreated pain often leads a person to move less and gain weight, for example, or to shift balance in unnatural ways, increasing the chance of falling and breaking a bone.

Editors Feature

Treatments and surgery is considered part of and for many women and men the thought of hair loss or any other results from treatment can be draining. Its important to keep a good mind healthy body and most of all to keep your friends and family's close. Strong relationships come out even stronger.

Check out these sites that will help get you and your loved ones the kind of information that can help you.

Www.mayoclinic.com
Www.cancer.org
Www.beatlivertumors.org
Www.bannerhealth.com

Editors Feature

His First Kiss; How to be his first

On the first night of the first date you want to go over the old check list. Did you wear deodorant, brush your teeth, chose the right mint, so on and so fourth. But when it comes time to worrying about the first kiss should that be your set back? We think not, so here we investigate why and how first kiss can make or break your new relationship.

When your ready and you feel its right make your self kissable, try some gloss light scented, keep your breath fresh and always wear a light scented smell. These tangible accessories she will appreciate. The next thing is making eye contact. You want to lean in on her shoulder then lay your head closer as if to signal for her to move in. You want to give her subtle hints like looking at her lips while slowly dropping your eyes to give him a subtle eye gaze. Reach up to twine your hands around her and lean in face to face to get that romantic mood.

If you feel like she is hesitant offer her a invitation. See if she would respond to something like " Could we just be kissing right now?" This will let her know that you want to try new things or even more. Always be polite and always be gentle.

Remember this is your guys first kiss so you don't want to be nervous just trust your feelings and go with the flow.

The World of Entertainment

TOP PICKS OF THIS MONTH.....

Concealed in Death
By: JD Roberts
The incomparable J. D. Robb presents the latest moving and suspenseful novel in the #1 New York Times bestselling Eve Dallas series. In a decrepit, long-empty New York building, Lieutenant Eve Dallas's husband begins the demolition process by swinging a sledgehammer into a wall. When the dust clears, there are two skeletons wrapped in plastic behind it. He summons his wife immediately—and by the time .

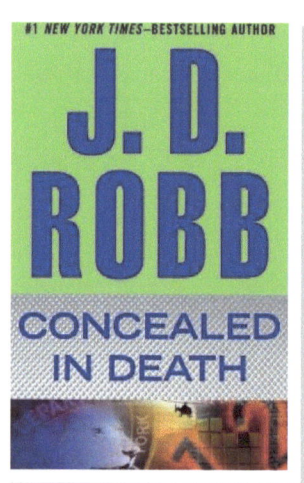

Stone Cold
By: C.J. Box

The electrifying new Joe Pickett novel from the New York Times bestselling author. Everything about the man is a mystery: the massive ranch in the remote Black Hills of Wyoming that nobody ever visits, the women who live with him, the secret philanthropies, the private airstrip, the sudden disappearances. And especially the persistent rumors that the man's wealth comes from killing people.

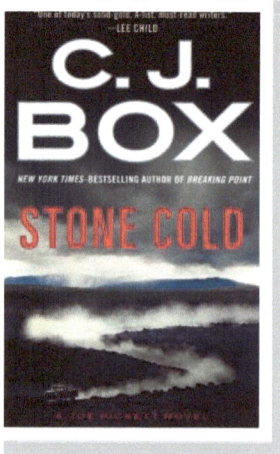

Doggy's World
Music Events:

U.S. Airways Center Presents

Marquee Theatre Presents

Phoenix Suns VS LA Clippers
April 2

Disney on Ice: 100 Years of Magic
April 10

Spanish Speaking Performance: Disney on Ice 100 Years of Magic

Dark Star Orchestra
April 3

Elle Goulding
April 9

Broken Bells
April 10

201 E Jefferson St. Phoenix, AZ 85004 602-379-7878

730 N Mill Ave, Tempe AZ 85281, 480-829-0607

Fashion No or not....
Brought to you by: Lisabeths Design

Active wear what to actually wear

When your working out you want to wear things that are loose and flexible and form fitting or not. Most people don't want to wear something to tight and some people do, that's all your own personal preference. But here is what we suggest;

When your working out it really depends on your style most like the yoga pants. I do and here is a few things about them.

According to Wikipedia...

Yoga pants are a type of flexible, form-fitting pants designed for the practice of yoga as well as other activities that involve a lot of movement, bending and stretching. Some of the other activities include: martial arts, dancing, Pilates, aerobics, clubbing, etc. These pants are generally made of cotton, spandex, nylon, polyester or a similarly light and stretchy synthetic material. They are usually black, tight-fitted, and have an elastic waistband folded over at the top. Although designed specifically for yoga, the pants are also worn casually by many women

So .... we know that they move with your body and compliment them too.

Now Choose your top........

Your top is one of two parts, Your sports bra which is like a bra but better. Probably the original...lol....but really its made to hold you in while your running or doing your routine. Next is the shirt. Its really your choice from cotton t shirts to tight stretch fleece or tanks. So when you choose go for style and color you'll have more fun and enjoy your workout more.

DESIGN SEO STYLE CREATE SEO LIFE

As one of the leading technology gadgets we see everything getting smaller and smaller. Hence the old saying look at it from far away and it's just a mirage. The times of technology is focusing on handy , newer, and more information. The more information you can get in a smaller look the better. So we would want to incorporate this concept into our own version.

With all of our prices we still stand behind packages. Our basic package is the $55 for everything and 200 copies. From this we added simple things like print publication opportunities to advertising on our online sites and social sites that brings your business closer to other business. We have also added promotion and events. This means that we are able to enhance your business through promotions, specials email marketing campaigns or new products. We're also able to keep the word of mouth going with events. This means that we can put together a marketable event that would get you out there. Theses include outsourcing for any types of agendas we can. Think of it as the RSVP of your event.

Finally back to our perspective drawing boards, we want to be a small handy but effective means in your budget. Yet we also know that we can bring big awareness.

From our friends at Wikipedia..... TECHNOLOGY

Alice Cooperstown

Enjoy Great food and exciting entertainment coming from the heart of Phoenix Arizona !

Check out some rave reviews from some of its own!

You can get anything you want, at Alice's restaurant....Had out of town guests and we went there on a weekday. Arrived just as they opened at 11 and were immediately greeted by hostess and seated. Loved the "decor" and spent several minutes (well, actually quite a while) checking it out. Yeah, it's similar style to the Hard Rock Cafe, but that's to be expected. As for the food, well it was plentiful, delicious and fair priced. I had Cooper's Turkey Sliders and they were awesome. I really liked everything about the place and despite the 30 min drive will be back often (esp. when we have visitors or go to the Sky Harbor). Location is perfect for before or after a Diamondback or Suns game. Awesome classic rock playing made it even better! One suggestion: this place would be even more fun if the staff looked like they enjoyed their jobs. Not a lot of smiles or friendly small talk.

Alice Cooperstown
101 E Jackson St
Phoenix AZ 85034

Pablo Ruiz y Picasso, known as Pablo Picasso (Spanish: [ˈpaβlo piˈkaso]; 25 October 1881 – 8 April 1973) was a Spanish painter, sculptor, printmaker, ceramicist, stage designer, poet and playwright who spent most of his adult life in France. As one of the greatest and most influential artists of the 20th century, he is known for co-founding the Cubist movement, the invention of constructed sculpture,[2][3] the co-invention of collage, and for the wide variety of styles that he helped develop and explore. Among his most famous works are the proto-Cubist Les Demoiselles d'Avignon (1907), and Guernica (1937), a portrayal of the German bombing of Guernica during the Spanish Civil War.

Picasso, Henri Matisse and Marcel Duchamp are regarded as the three artists who most defined the revolutionary developments in the plastic arts in the opening decades of the 20th century, responsible for significant developments in painting, sculpture, printmaking and ceramics

Trendy News What You Want To Know

Chris Brown out of Rehab

Singer Chris Brown has been booted from court-ordered drug rehab and taken into custody by Los Angeles County Sheriff's deputies, a sheriff's spokesman confirmed Friday.

Details were not immediately available about why Brown, 24, was kicked out of the Malibu facility where he has been treated for the past four months.

Nor was it clear exactly why he was taken into immediate custody, but he had been serving a five-year probation sentence when he entered rehab. That sentence stemmed from a 2009 assault on then-girlfriend Rihanna

Comedian David Brenner, 'Tonight' favorite, dies

LOS ANGELES (AP) — David Brenner, the lanky, toothy-grinned "Tonight Show" favorite whose brand of observational comedy became a staple for other standups, including Jerry Seinfeld and Paul Reiser, died Saturday. He was 78.

Brenner, who had been fighting cancer, died peacefully at his home in New York City with his family at his side, according to Jeff Abraham, his friend and publicist.

New Technology For The Modern Geek

Lekani trendy heart shape new gadgets 2014 N493

This trendy heart necklace is one to shop and buy for your special someone. This trendy necklace is gold plated available with crystal rhinestone. Check website for details.

www.alibaba.com

Road Tested Chair

There's nothing pedestrian about this chair. Artisan John Carter combines fine art, interior design and social commentary for a truly one-of-a-kind creation. The New York City "Walk/Don't Walk" signs actually work - and a remote control is included to turn them on and off. The legs are made from reconfigured, customized steel street sign brackets, with galvanized, heavy duty self-leveling feet.

New Technology Vs. The other guys

The human species' use of technology began with the conversion of natural resources into simple tools. The prehistorically discovery of the ability to control fire increased the available sources of food and the invention of the wheel helped humans in travelling in and controlling their environment. Recent technological developments, including the printing press, the telephone, and the Internet, have lessened physical barriers to communication and allowed humans to interact freely on a global scale. However, not all technology has been used for peaceful purposes; the development of weapons of ever-increasing destructive power has progressed throughout history, from clubs to nuclear weapons.

Technology has affected society and its surroundings in a number of ways. In many societies, technology has helped develop more advanced economies (including today's global economy) and has allowed the rise of a leisure class. Many technological processes produce unwanted by-products, known as pollution, and deplete natural resources, to the detriment of Earth's environment. Various implementations of technology influence the values of a society and new technology often raises new ethical questions. Examples include the rise of the notion of efficiency in terms of human productivity, a term originally applied only to machines, and the challenge of traditional norms.

Philosophical debates have arisen over the present and future use of technology in society, with disagreements over whether technology improves the human condition or worsens it. Neo-Luddism, anarchy-primitivism, and similar movements criticize the pervasiveness of technology in the modern world, opining that it harms the environment and alienates people; proponents of ideologies such as trans humanism and techno-progressivism view continued technological progress as beneficial to society and the human condition. Indeed, until recently, it was believed that the development of technology was restricted only to human beings, but recent scientific studies indicate that other primates and certain dolphin communities have developed simple tools and learned to pass their knowledge to other

Enhancement

Human enhancement refers to any attempt to temporarily or permanently overcome the current limitations of the human body through natural or artificial means. The term is sometimes applied to the use of technological means to select or alter human characteristics and capacities, whether or not the alteration results in characteristics and capacities that lie beyond the existing human range. Here, the test is whether the technology

In scientific usage, a phenomenon is any event that is observable, however common it might be, even if it requires the use of instrumentation to observe, record, or compile data concerning it. For example, in physics, a phenomenon may be a feature of matter, energy, or space-time, such as Isaac Newton's observations of the moon's orbit and of gravity, or Galileo Galilee's observations of the motion of a pendulum.[4] Another example of scientific phenomena can be found in the experience of phantom limb sensations. This occurrence, the sensation of feeling in amputated limbs, is reported by over 70% of amputees. Although the limb is no longer present, they report still experiencing sensations. This is an extraordinary event that defies typical logic and has been a source of much curiosity within the medical and physiological fields

In recent decades, a new possibility for LGBT parenting, same-sex procreation (where two women could have a daughter with equal genetic contributions from both women, or where two men could have a son or daughter with equal genetic contributions from both men), has become a possibility, through the creation of either female sperm or male eggs from the cells of adult women and men. With female sperm and male eggs, lesbian and gay couples wishing to become parents would not have to rely on a third party donor of sperm or egg.

Social apps and more
Find us !

The online world

Business Watch: What We Need To Know

<u>Rob Ford's Brother Has Beef With Kevin Spacey</u>

Embattled Toronto Mayor Rob Ford's brother, Doug, said he thinks actor Kevin Spacey is an "arrogant S.O.B." in the latest episode of the "Ford Nation" podcast co-hosted by the siblings.

Doug, who is a city councilor in Toronto, was upset with Spacey for allegedly declining to take photos with people when they were both backstage at the taping of Mayor Ford's appearance on "Jimmy Kimmel Live" earlier this month.

"There was this Kevin Spacey OK? I want to start off with saying Kevin Spacey is an incredible actor," Doug began.
"I don't watch movies," Rob interjected. "I wouldn't know him if I ran him over."
Doug went on to describe being shunned by Spacey.
"In my opinion he's an arrogant S.O.B. and I'll tell you the reason why," recounted Doug. "Any actor that makes a living off the people that watch his shows, he wouldn't take a picture with anyone? We were told you can't take a picture and you can't speak to him. Who does this character think he is?"
"I don't even know him," Rob replied.
Doug then offered some unsolicited advice for Spacey.

"He thinks he's god, that he's up there, that no common folk can take a picture," Doug declared. "So, you know Kevin, why don't you get off your high horse and be real and take pictures with people?"
Business Insider emailed Doug to ask if he'd received an apology from Spacey after the podcast debuted Friday. Doug did not immediately respond.
Watch the full clip below.

Survive The Realestate Market

Is a Home Warranty Worth the Cost?

Whether you are buying your first home or selling a home and moving into another, a home warranty could be a valuable protection for your finances and your peace of mind. Many buyers opt to purchase home warranties, which average $350 to $500 for a basic warranty and $100 to $300 more for a warranty with extra protection. Buyers, particularly first-time buyers, like the fact that they can rely on a warranty to pay for repairs during the first year while they are settling into a new home. In some cases, a real estate agent will purchase a home warranty for the buyers as a settlement gift or thank-you for their business. Home sellers, particularly if they are selling a home with older appliances and systems, can purchase a one-year warranty that will protect them while their place is on the market and can then be transferred along with ownership of the house to their buyers. Not only does the home warranty provide an extra incentive for buyers who are concerned about potential costly repairs, but it is available for the sellers in case a water heater, oven or some other appliance needs to be fixed.

Read more at:

http://www.realtor.com/advice/home-warranty-worth-cost/

Politics: Special Feature

Malaysia Airlines Flight 370 search grows as pilots face increased scrutiny

Where do you even begin to look, when the search area covers vast swaths of land and water, stretching thousands of miles, from Kazakhstan to the Indian Ocean?

That's the question for Malaysian officials and authorities from 24 other nations as people search for a ninth day, trying to find Malaysia Airlines Flight 370 and the 239 people on board.

As the search area grows bigger, authorities are also increasing their scrutiny of the pilots, searching their homes in the quest for clues. That included a flight simulator from the captain's home.

North Korea fires short-range rockets,

North Korea has fired 10 short-range rockets, two South Korean defense officials said Sunday.

The rockets were fired from the eastern coast of the Korean peninsula toward the Sea of Japan, according to the officials, who asked not to be identified by name as a matter of security protocol.

"We estimate the rockets traveled about 70 kilometers in the open waters," one of the officials said.

Such actions have drawn criticism from South Korea and the West.

The U.S. State Department said it's aware of the reports of rocket launches by North Korea and is closely monitoring the situation

Spain arrests 7 suspected of sending militant fighters to Syria

Police in Spain and Morocco arrested seven suspected Islamist militants who recruited and sent fighters for al Qaeda terrorist organizations in Syria and Mali, Spain's Interior Ministry said Friday.

The suspects include a Spaniard and two Frenchmen who were arrested in the Spanish enclave of Melilla on Morocco's north coast, a Tunisian arrested in the city of Malaga on the Spanish mainland and three Moroccans detained in Morocco, the ministry said.

A ministry statement said it was, to date, "the most important" breaking of a cell said to be involved in sending Islamic militant fighters to Syria.

Politics Transformed

THE ONLINE BATTLE FOR YOUR VOTE

Politics: The who and what of Politics

Sleep Loss the affects

Are you a truck driver or shift worker planning to catch up on some sleep this weekend?

Cramming in extra hours of shut-eye may not make up for those lost pulling all-nighters, new research indicates.

The damage may already be done -- brain damage, that is, said neuroscientist Sigrid Veasey from the University of Pennsylvania.

Alzheimer's & Sleep

The widely held idea that you can pay back a sizeable "sleep debt" with long naps later on seems to be a myth, she said in a study published this week in the Journal of Neuroscience.

Long-term sleep deprivation saps the brain of power even after days of recovery sleep, Veasey said. And that could be a sign of lasting brain injury.

Hilary Clinton: Putin its up to you if there is a Cold War!

Hillary Clinton said on Tuesday that the conflict between Russia and Western allies over Crimea is a "clash of values" and that it's up to Russian President Vladimir Putin whether there's "another Cold War."

"I hope there is not another Cold War," Clinton said during the question and answer portion of an appearance in Montreal. "Obviously, nobody wants to see that. I think that is primarily up to Putin."

Rob Ford Caught !

Rob Ford caught outside of the convention center drinking. Was reportedly with friends while boozing it up and making obscured remarks toward the locals and the reporters. While getting into a car and going toward a undisclosed location. Mayor Rob Ford who was caught smoking crack and with a prostitute is said to be in control of his emotional state.

2014 MARCH

SUNDAY	MONDAY	TUESDAY	WEDNESDAY	THURSDAY	FRIDAY	SATURDAY
						1
2	3	4	5	6	7	8
9	10	11	12	13	14	15
16	17	18	19	20	21	22
23	24	25	26	27	28	29
30	31					

This month will be a great month!
April Has Arrived

Join our mailing list and get a free 1 month Subscription to our magazine! www.lisabethdesignm agazine.com

Owner

Design & Concepts L.L.C

Elizabeth Chavez
602-785-1108

Creativedesignconcepts@rocketmail.com

Place orders by email or contact

BE CREATIVE.GO OUT AND DESIGN SOMETHING

Design & Concepts

House of Lisabeths Design Magazine
We were started in 2013 as an independent magazine. Our focus is fashion, health
and business. We pride ourselves in the design and diversity we offer.
Exclusivity
Our focus is fashion , health and business. Our fashion section includes tips and
trends from all over! We also have a online blog that gets tons of clicks per day, check
us out online at ....
Our business section is used for local or national business to place a Ad or listing of
them selfs. We have total exclusivity In that they connect with not only our magazine
but all of our networks simultaneously.
Our hope is to reach across the world along with Water 4 Kids International.
We plan to donate proceeds to this foundation. Our hope is to provide safe water for
east Africa.
Check us out on line, Facebook, Twitter, Tumblr, Amazon, and our affiliates websites
like Design & Concepts.

Get a 1 year subscription for $ 35.00——————— ☐
—

Get a 2 Year Subscription for $ 45.00——————— ☐
—

☐

Payment Enclosed————————————.

☐

Charge My Card————————————.

☐

Pay Later————————————————.

Send To:

Design & Concepts
32 e Ruth Ave # 304
Phoenix, Arizona 85020

We also take check, cash and money orders.

Remember when you send for a subscription you get a free
t-shirt that says "Lisabeth Design"

Thanks for supporting our fashion blog and Section!

Personal Info

Name:
_____

Address:
_____
_

City, State, Zip:
_____
_____

Credit Card Info:
_Visa ☐
Master-   ☐ Card
AMEX   ☐

Card Number:
_____

Expiration Date:
_____

3 number code:
_____

" Fill out above info and return to address
given"

Available for Men and Women

Check out Design & Concepts Blog

DONT BUY MEAT
The worthy of the worth and the Elite of the Elite make a
common general statement. " DONT BUY MEAT!" You may
ask what dose this mean, no meat no nothing don't buy it if
its not out there for a good reason or a beneficial reason
don't buy it. I once took a seminar on how you can here 100
things at a time and not understand everything that you are
listening to. For instance a commercial can advertise the
same tactics, like hey we have this new and improve staple,
but yet what is going to make you buy this new and improve
staple in the first place. Putting away your needs and obvi-
ous i just so happened to lose my normal staple. You start
to realize that you don't need the automatic closer, the quick
throw back metal thing that snaps back faster then any other staple after you squeeze. You just need a super awesome
staple. A staple the thing of necessity. So by saying this i
again , build networks and offer professional opportunities.
limitations of the human body through natural or artificial
means. The term is sometimes applied to the use of technological means to select or alter human characteristics and
capacities, whether or not the alteration results in characteristics and capacities that lie beyond the existing human

Join the Cause!
Check out the " Design for Sick Kids Campaign"

Our Mission
In the beginning we wanted a way to show our passion for design.
But this project is turning to be more then that. With so many sick
kids and so much that we can give we thought about giving the gift
of design.

What We Need & What You Get
Here is what we need
1000 cards , either designed by you or who ever
A contribution as well to our campaign

The Impact
With every card made we will donate a dollar and that card to a local
hospital of our choice. So think about all the kids you can help by
creating there Christmas card or birthday card and also the contri-
butions that come with it.
Remember every card made we donate $ 1.00 to the cause
Also share your design with the people and get your picture taken
with the kids

Other Ways You Can Help Check out our websites
www.designandconcepts.net for more updates on more causes!

http://www.indiegogo.com/projects/design-a-card-for-your-kids/

Also with your subscription get a free Lisabeth Design T- Shirt

Available for Men and Women

Design & Concepts Services

Www.Designandconcepts.net
Www.lisabethdesignmagazine.com

Design & Concepts is an online service provider for design and advertising. We specialize in brochures logos and business cards as well as t shirts and sickies. We also do local advertising with in the community. Our prices vary with design but...

Our packages start at $55.00 per package!
Package includes : 200 prints
Gloss or matt finish is $10.00 per set/ per 200

Our Packages also include our Marketing Services, and Discounts on our Advertising Specials in our magazine, House of Lisabeth De-

Also with your subscription get a free Lisabeth Design T- Shirt

Available for Men and Women

Design & Concepts Services:

Create various ads and place it on all social networks, web pages and create you tube videos to sell, demonstrate and promote your product

Also place your ad on any media source that is available We can take your campaign and place it on any other media resources you have available not just create a web presence awareness but really hit the market.

.We use digital media like

Email marketing, social network campaigns, print distribution, custom Web Design and SEO

Economic costs[edit]

The economic costs of managing waste are high, and are often paid for by municipal governments;[10] money can often be saved with more efficiently designed collection routes, modifying vehicles, and with public education. Environmental policies such as pay as you throw can reduce the cost of management and reduce waste quantities. Waste recovery (that is, recycling, reuse) can curb economic costs because it avoids extracting raw materials and often cuts transportation costs. "Economic assessment of municipal waste management systems – case studies using a combination of life cycle assessment (LCA) and life cycle costing (LCC)". Journal of Cleaner Production 13 (2005): 253-263.</ref> The location of waste treatment and disposal facilities often has an impact on property values due to noise, dust, pollution, unsightliness, and negative stigma. The informal waste sector consists mostly of waste pickers who scavenge for metals, glass, plastic, textiles, and other materials and then trade them for a profit. This sector can significantly alter or reduce waste in a particular system, but other negative economic effects come with the disease, poverty, exploitation, and abuse of its workers

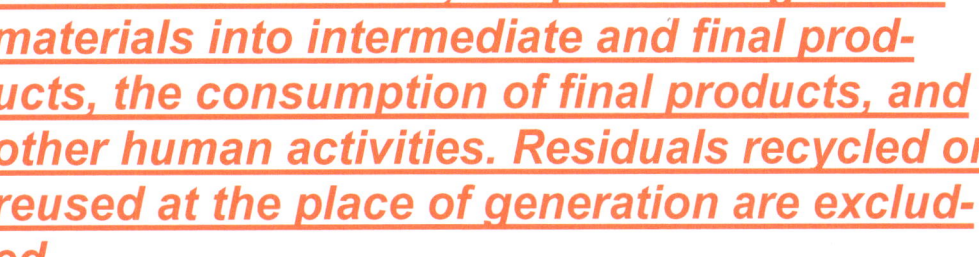

"Wastes are materials that are not prime products (that is products produced for the market) for which the initial user has no further use in terms of his/her own purposes of production, transformation or consumption, and of which he/she wants to dispose. Wastes may be generated during the extraction of raw materials, the processing of raw materials into intermediate and final products, the consumption of final products, and other human activities. Residuals recycled or reused at the place of generation are excluded

Recipe Of The Month

Meat and Mushroom Lasagna

Ingredients

1 tablespoon olive oil
2 cloves garlic, minced
1 onion, diced
2 tablespoons tomato paste
2 teaspoons ground oregano
1 teaspoon ground basil
1/4 teaspoon ground fennel
8 ounces portabella mushrooms, chopped
Pinch red pepper flakes
1 1/2 pounds ground chuck
1/4 teaspoon salt
1/4 teaspoon pepper
One 14.5-ounce can diced tomatoes with basil, garlic and oregano
One 15-ounce can tomato sauce
1 1/4 cups grated Parmigiano-Reggiano
1 cup small curd cottage cheese
One 8-ounce package part-skim shredded mozzarella cheese
1 large egg, lightly beaten
2 tablespoons freshly chopped parsley leaves
Zest of 1 lemon
9 whole-wheat oven-ready noodles

Directions

Heat the olive oil in a large saucepan and then add the garlic and onions and cook until softened, about 5 minutes. Stir in the tomato paste, oregano, basil and fennel, and then add the mushrooms and red pepper flakes. Stir in the ground beef and cook over medium heat until browned and crumbled. Add tomatoes and tomato sauce, bring to a boil, and then reduce the heat and simmer for 40 to 45 minutes.

Preheat the oven to 350 degrees F.

Mix together the Parmigiano-Reggiano, cottage cheese, 2/3 cup of mozzarella and the egg in a small bowl. Stir in the parsley and lemon zest.

Spoon one-quarter of the sauce into the bottom of a 13- by 9- by 2-inch baking pan.

Place 3 uncooked lasagna noodles on top of the sauce without overlapping. Spread half of the cottage cheese mixture over noodles and top with another one-quarter of the sauce. Repeat the layers, ending with sauce, and sprinkle over the remaining mozzarella cheese.

Bake for 45 minutes. Let rest 10 minutes before serving.

Classifieds

Office Management
Office Team
Qualifications:
• Customer Service and Administrative skills.
• 2+ years of experience – non managerial.
• College/University degrees not required.
• Extra Curricular activities: e.g. University (student organizations, athletics etc.).
• Working Knowledge of Office Administrative functions and software such as Microsoft office products.
 You may submit your application materials online or call 1.800.804.8367 for additional ways to apply.

AT&T
Sales Support Representative
Customer service experience, store operations,

Perform the following with reasonable accommodation:
Work flexible hours (including evenings, weekends and holidays)
Stand for long periods of time
 Ability to lift up to 25 pounds
Operate a personal computer, wireless equipment, copier and fax
 Work in other locations as the needs of the business dictate what may be required
May be required to wear a uniform or company apparel as designated by management

Apply : www.at&t/careers.com

Spectrum Brand
Seasonal Merchandising Associates

Responsible for servicing, merchandising, and promoting the sale of company's consumer packaged goods products within established national retail accounts in assigned territory. Additionally this position is responsible for building consumer loyalty by assisting consumers in selecting products appropriate to their need, through asking questions, listening, recommending products and influencing the sale

Apply: http://www.spectrumbrands.com/

Showcase Honda
Experience Auto Sales Rep

As a highly-valued employee of Showcase Honda, you will be offered a highly competitive compensation package that includes everything from insurance and retirement benefits to bonuses and discounts.

Our employees are offered medical, dental, vision, life, short and long-term disability, and workers compensation insurance; a 401K plan; and paid vacation. You also will have access to discounts on parts, clothing, maintenance work and even cars.

Showcase Honda
1333 East Camelback Rd
Phoenix, AZ 85014

Direct Energy
Sales Manager

Phoenix call center , Fulltime , looking for sales and marketing . Also management sales 8-10 years experience, requirered.   Proven ability to work well in a high pressure/target driven environment

Work Environment (circle one below)
Office setting, Field Services, Production Work, etc

Apply:

http://directenergy.taleo.net/careersection

Arizona Team
Business Administration Supervisor & Management Position

Assisting our clients in the retention and acquisition of business customers

Supervising and coaching account managers and account executives.
Learning the business aspect of running a marketing firm
All business & communication aspects in between our clients and their target market

Apply:

www.arizona-team.com

John C Lincoln
Desert Mission Practice Administrator

This individual will provide overall administrative direction and coordination of ambulatory clinic service activities and programs of a health center site including assurance that all medical equipment and all other physical properties are maintained and are in good operational condition. Has responsibility for the planning, development, organization coordination, fiduciary responsibility as well as integration and evaluation of medical services. Effectively plans and directs center operations by coordinating business office and clinical activities to achieve maximum expense control and productivity of staff and physicians. This position reports directly to the Executive Director.

Apply:

www-healthcaresource-com.careerliaison.com

Krispy Kreme Doughnuts
Shift Supervisor

We are currently seeking Top Performing Shift Supervisors for a Top Performing Company to ensure the continued growth of our business. We are looking for people with a proven track record, seeking personal growth opportunity, who enjoy working with people and get excited about providing outstanding customer service

Full time, $10-12 per hour

Apply:

www.krispykreme.com/Careers/Info

__Looking for classifieds, if interested submit your business and information and well help you out!__

__Liz:__
__creativedesignconcepts@rocketmail.com__